W9-BPJ-260

Finding Sunshine After the Storm

A Workbook for Children Healing from Sexual Abuse

SHARON A. M^CGEE, LMFT
CURTIS HOLMES, PH.D.

Instant Help Books
A Division of New Harbinger Publications, Inc.

Publisher's Note

This publication is designed to provide accurate and authoritative information in regard to the subject matter covered. It is sold with the understanding that the publisher is not engaged in rendering psychological, financial, legal, or other professional services. If expert assistance or counseling is needed, the services of a competent professional should be sought.

Distributed in Canada by Raincoast Books

Copyright © 2008 by Sharon McGee and Curtis Holmes
  Instant Help Books
  A Division of New Harbinger Publications, Inc.
  5674 Shattuck Avenue
  Oakland, CA 94609
  www.newharbinger.com

Cover design by Amy Shoup

All rights reserved

Printed in the United States of America

Library of Congress Cataloging-in-Publication Data on file with publisher

16   15   14

10   9   8   7   6   5   4

Contents

A Note to Adults

Sexual abuse is always a trauma for children, and it is also traumatic for the adults who care for the child. Most parents and even many professional counselors don't know where to begin in helping children recover from sexual abuse, but this workbook, written by two highly experienced therapists, will help focus on the power of children to recover and heal.

Finding Sunshine After the Storm will inspire new thoughts, feelings, and behaviors in children by using activities that kids will find both familiar and reassuring. Each activity is a building block that children can use to focus on their positive attributes and to understand their own complex feelings.

The activities in this workbook can be used in counseling sessions or as "therapeutic homework" between counseling sessions. They will help children learn to express their anger in appropriate ways, become better problem solvers, be aware of dangerous situations, and much more.

Each activity in the workbook teaches children a new emotional or behavioral skill, but all skills much be practiced and reinforced. Children who have been sexually abused have unique emotional needs, and certainly not all children have the same needs. But all children benefit from the positive support and guidance of adults, and this should always be your first concern. The activities in this book are wonderful tools to help children heal, but healing does not come from any book; it comes in the context of warm and supportive relationships.

As you help a child with the activities in this book, you will probably find out that it is difficult for children to talk about certain issues. Never force a child to talk if he or she doesn't want to. The best way to get children to open up is to be a good role model. Talk about *your* thoughts, feelings, and experiences as they relate to each activity, stressing the positive ways that *you* cope with problems. Even if a child doesn't say a thing back, your words will have an impact on his or her behavior.

As you use this workbook, you must always remember to remain patient and respectful of a child's feelings. Many adults have a tendency to want to put difficult feelings and experiences in the past, but children need to lead the way toward their own healing. Fortunately, most children have a great capacity for growth and self-acceptance. Your time and caring will make all the difference.

Sincerely,

Lawrence Shapiro, PhD

Introduction

We like the rain, but we don't like big bad thunderstorms. Eventually, things do calm down. The sun comes out, and after storms, everything looks so sparkly and clean. But, sometimes, it's hard to wait for that to happen.

We all need to realize just how strong we are inside, and we need to have helpers in our lives because nobody deserves to go through tough times by themselves. Some things may have happened to you that have been pretty tough, but you are super strong inside and you have some great people helping you out—and that makes all the difference.

This book is about finding the sunshine after the storms: learning how to see the good things in life again and seeing the GREAT things about you.

—The Authors

Paste a picture of yourself in the space below.

My name is _____

My friends call me _____

I am _____ years old.

The school I go to is _____

My brothers' and sisters' names and ages are _____

_____

One thing I REALLY like to do is _____

_____

One thing I REALLY don't like to do is _____

_____

I wish _____

_____

If I had a day to do anything I wanted, I would _____

_____

and I would want _____ to be there with me.

One thing I think I am really great at doing is _____

_____

One thing my friends say they like about me is _____

_____

One thing I wish no one knew about me is _____

_____

One thing I wish EVERYBODY knew about me is _____

_____

Things I Am Proud Of

Using your favorite color crayon or marker, circle all the things on this page that you like about yourself.

I am a good helper.

I like what I see when I look in the mirror.

I can run really fast.

I can make people laugh.

I can dance.

People like me.

I am good at cleaning.

I like the way I sing.

I am smart.

I try hard.

I am a good friend.

I am learning to talk about my feelings.

Things I Am Proud Of

On the lines below, write more things that make you feel proud of yourself.

_____	_____	_____
_____	_____	_____
_____	_____	_____
_____	_____	_____
_____	_____	_____
_____	_____	_____
_____	_____	_____
_____	_____	_____
_____	_____	_____
_____	_____	_____
_____	_____	_____
_____	_____	_____
_____	_____	_____
_____	_____	_____
_____	_____	_____
_____	_____	_____

Who Are My Helpers?

It is important to know the helpers in your life, so that you can ask them for help when you need it. It can be hard to ask for help, but all brave, strong kids know that helpers are important. And asking for help when you need it is the MOST important thing you can do!

Who are some people that have always been your helpers?

1. _____

2. _____

3. _____

4. _____

5. _____

Did you remember to put the helpers from your family on your list?

_____

You may have a lot of new helpers in your life now. These helpers do lots of different things, and one important thing they do is to help YOU!

Can you name some of the new helpers in your life?

1. _____

2. _____

3. _____

4. _____

5. _____

Remember, all these helpers are there to help you. Isn't it great to have so many helpers?

Have you ever heard the word "trauma"? A trauma is a really, really bad experience, which can make you feel so helpless and scared that you aren't even sure you will survive it. You may have had a trauma happen to you. Maybe someone touched your private parts in a way that was so awful or scary that you didn't know what was going to happen.

When you think about what happened, you may feel all the same scary and confusing feelings you felt then. Just reading these words, you might even feel those feelings. But thinking about the trauma is not the same as when it happened. You are safe reading these words; the trauma is not happening again.

You may also have noticed that you avoid thinking or talking about the trauma because you get some of those scary feelings back when you do. You may try to separate yourself from what happened by picturing it like a scene from a movie or by forgetting parts of it. You may feel nervous or jumpy. Some kids who have had a trauma even start to feel like they are crazy.

Here's the good news: you are not crazy. What you are feeling is the effect of going through a trauma. Here are some questions to ask yourself:

1. Can you remember clearly everything that happened? If you feel like you can't remember parts of what happened, tell your counselor.

2. Do you find yourself avoiding the subject—and then hiding the fact that you are avoiding it? Again, tell your therapist. You won't have to talk about the things you're avoiding right away, but it will help your therapist to help you.

3. Are you really moody? Again, tell your therapist. Together, you can try to figure out what causes your moods to change.

In the space below, draw a picture of a really, really crazy person.

Doesn't look like you, does it?

Here are some other things you can do to help yourself after a trauma.

How can each of these things help?

Get a good night's sleep.

_____

_____

_____

Have active fun.

_____

_____

_____

Laugh!

_____

_____

_____

Talk to a counselor.

_____

_____

_____

Eat good food.

_____

_____

_____

Find someone who cares about you.

_____

_____

_____

My Worry Circle

When people are worried about something, they usually think about it a lot. They think of all the bad things about it and wonder about what may happen. Usually, worrying doesn't help solve problems, but it's still hard to stop. It's sort of like cleaning up spilled juice—you think you've wiped it all up, but your feet keep sticking to the floor.

Everybody worries sometimes—even kids. You might worry about things like school, your friends, your family, or what happened to you.

First, think of the things you worry about. Then, think of things grown-ups tell you to stop worrying about or thinking about all the time. Write all these thing inside your worry circle.

My Worry Circle

The best way to help deal with worries is to talk about them. Once you have written your worries in your worry circle, talk to your counselor about them. Your counselor can help you figure them out and talk to your family about them if you need to.

Which kids do you think work better at school and behave better at home: kids who like themselves or kids who don't?

You're right! Usually, kids who like themselves do better in all sorts of ways. So the great news is that the more you practice liking yourself, the better you will feel AND the better you will do in school and at home. Once you are done with this activity, take a bow. When musicians have finished playing really well, they bow and smile while the audience cheers and claps. Remember to do that when you have finished this activity!

When people like themselves, they have what is called "high self-esteem." Other people like to be with them because they are usually cheerful, and they believe in themselves. They have more fun and they often are confident that they can find things to do that they are good at.

If you have high self-esteem or want to have high self-esteem, raise your right hand!

Some people have high self-esteem because everything has gone pretty well in their lives. It never occurs to them not to believe in themselves, because everyone else believes in them. Other people have high self-esteem because they work hard at it. Some parts of their lives may have gone well and some not. Some people have treated them well and some haven't, but they have high self-esteem because they have learned how to believe in themselves!

Here are some ways people can build their self-esteem:

- ☐ By concentrating on positive thoughts about themselves

- ☐ By forgiving themselves for making mistakes

- ☐ By finding friends who treat them well

- ☐ By reminding themselves that they are capable, lovable, and worthwhile

On the pages that follow, you'll find some things to write and draw about that will help you practice liking yourself.

People who have high self-esteem look for things they are good at, but they don't have to be good at everything. Everyone is different, and it's okay that some kids are better than other kids at certain skills. After all, there are some things that you are better at than most other kids.

In the space below, draw a picture of some things you are good at.

Were you always good at these things, or did you practice them to get better and better at them?

_____

_____

_____

_____

_____

Do you have a best friend?

In the space below, draw what you think your best friend likes most about you.

Write about what you were thinking while you were drawing this picture.

_____

_____

_____

_____

_____

One of the most important things you can do to have high self-esteem is to be careful about the things you think and say about yourself. Remember not to think or say mean things about yourself out loud or in your head. Instead, think and say encouraging and positive things that make you feel confident and happy.

How many positive things can you think of to say to yourself? Write them here:

1. _____

2. _____

3. _____

4. _____

5. _____

6. _____

7. _____

8. _____

9. _____

10. _____

Now, if you're ready, stand up and take a bow!

Nice Job!

GREAT!

Way to Go!

Knew you could do it!

What to Do with an Inside Hurt

Have you ever fallen off your bike and scraped your knee? Even things that are fun to do can lead to a hurt or two. Did you park your bike and never ride again? No, you probably got back on and rode home to wash your knee off and put on a bandage or two.

What to Do with an Inside Hurt

Have you ever thought about how people can get hurt on the inside as well as on the outside? When someone hurts your feelings or when someone you love dies, those are inside hurts. Other things can cause inside hurts too, like bad touches or secret touches. Think about where you might have inside hurts. Maybe your head hurts because you think a lot about what happened. Or maybe you feel like your heart hurts because of something that happened.

On the picture below, draw bandages on all the places where you feel hurt inside.

On the lines below, write about your inside hurts.

_____

_____

_____

_____

_____

_____

_____

_____

_____

_____

_____

_____

_____

_____

_____

What to Do with an Inside Hurt

When you cut or scrape yourself, you help the hurt heal by keeping it clean and, perhaps, putting medicine on it.

On the lines below, tell what you can do to help an inside hurt get better.

_____

_____

_____

Outside hurts can take time to heal, and you have to take good care of them. Inside hurts can take time to heal as well, and you have to take care of them too.

Who are some people that can help you take care of your inside hurts?

1. _____

2. _____

3. _____

4. _____

5. _____

Did you know that you could help yourself by helping other people? A helper is someone who does something that helps another person. Moms and dads help their kids in many ways. Here are some things that parents do to help their kids:

- ☐ Fixing tasty and nutritious meals

- ☐ Doing the laundry

- ☐ Cleaning the house

- ☐ Reading to the kids at night

- ☐ Helping kids feel loved with hugs and words of love

- ☐ Supervising so everyone stays safe from harm

- ☐ Teaching good habits

- ☐ Being patient when mistakes are made

- ☐ Helping with homework

Kids can be helpers, too. But, believe it or not, there is a right way and a wrong way to be a helper. One wrong way to be a helper is to insist on helping the way you want to instead of giving the help the other person asks for.

Here's an example:

> Your mom asks you to clean the dining room table and you agree. Good for you! But what if you insist that you want to use the furniture polish, and you spray it on real thick, even on the glass parts of the table? Furniture polish doesn't usually make glass clean; it makes it kind of smeary. What if your mom explained the problem to you and asked you not to use so much polish, but you insisted on doing it your own way? Would that be a good way to help?

Some kids feel they have to grow up quickly and take care of themselves, because they aren't sure anyone else will do a good job taking care of them. These kids may start helping at a young age, but sometimes in a way that is NOT a good idea. *The Story of Rose* tells about that kind of help.

The Story of Rose

Once upon a time, a baby girl named Rose was born in a town near where you live. Her mother named her Rose because roses were her favorite kind of flower. Sadly, as Rose grew up, there were many problems in her family. First, her mom and dad got divorced. Because her dad did not understand how important he was to Rose, he didn't spend much time with her. Then, her mom started to use drugs because she was unhappy and thought the drugs would help her feel better. Rose's mom started paying more attention to her drugs then she did to her daughter. She didn't always clean the house when she should have, and she didn't even remember to feed Rose on time.

Rose was too young to understand about her mother's drug problem, but she did know she couldn't count on her mom to take care of her. As a result, little Rose started to try to take care of herself. When she was three, she even learned to fix her own cereal, so she would have something to eat every morning. She learned how to dress and feed herself, and how to find important stuff in the house. Once her mom had a big fight with her new boyfriend, and Rose even called 911 by herself.

Mom had another baby, and Rose now had a baby brother she called "Bubba." Before you know it, Rose was trying to take care of Bubba, too. She would get his bottle and pick him up to rock him when he cried. As Bubba and Rose got older, Rose would watch him to try to keep him safe, and she would spank him when he got into mischief.

One day, Mom's boyfriend tried to touch Rose in a way he wasn't supposed to. The next day, Rose told her teacher. A lady came to her school to ask her about what happened. By the end of the day, Rose and Bubba had gone to stay with their aunt, who was an excellent parent. She had two kids of her own, and she knew just how to take care of children. Suddenly, Rose found herself in a home where everything was done the best possible way for the kids, but she had a hard time stopping the way she had learned to help.

When her aunt said that Rose could just go play for a while longer, Rose tried to help her aunt cook supper. She tried to spank Bubba when he got into mischief, but her aunt told her not to act like she was Bubba's mother. Rose also wanted to listen when her aunt and uncle spoke privately about grown-up things, like paying bills and planning the family's schedule. Most importantly, Rose felt anxious and nervous all the time, like something else bad might happen at any minute. She had a hard time relaxing.

Well, time went by and soon Rose had lived with her aunt for two years. She was doing so much better. She learned to relax and to do what her aunt asked of her. And she learned more about how to be a kid and let the grown-ups be grown-ups.

Hooray for Rose!

Here are two important things to remember about being a helper:

- **When you want to help, you need to figure out what is actually helpful to the other person.**

- **Instead of trying to act like a grown-up, help grown-ups by letting them know you appreciate them.**

See if you can say or do any of these things in the next few days:

☐ During supper, tell the parent who cooked the meal that it tastes good and that you appreciate the work they did.

☐ When you get dressed to go to school, tell your parent how nice the fresh laundry smells.

☐ After having a story read to you, tell your parent you really like being read to and spending special time together.

☐ After your parent cleans up your house, say how great it looks.

☐ If your parent helps with your homework, say how much you appreciate the help.

Activity 9

Mirror, Mirror, on the Wall

When bad things happen, they can make you feel yucky inside. You may forget all the things that are great about you and only think about the things you don't like, or the things you want to change about yourself. The bad things anyone has ever said to you, or about you, just get stuck in your head and it's hard to get rid of them. Guess what? Most of those thoughts aren't even true!

In the fairy tale Snow White, do you remember when the Wicked Witch asked the mirror who was the fairest one of all? Imagine you have a special mirror that only shows you all the GREAT things about you. As you look into this mirror, ask yourself, "Mirror, mirror, on the wall, what great things about me do I recall?"

In the mirror on the next page, write all the great things you can think of about you—things you can do really well, things you like about who you are, things your friends and family like about you, and more. Think of as many things as you can so that your whole mirror is full of great things about you!

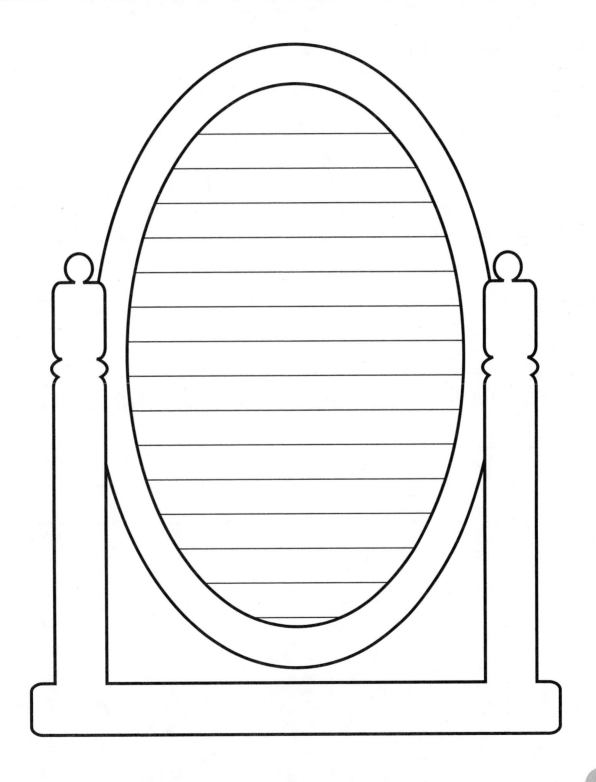

Next, answer these questions:

How did it feel to write all those great things about yourself?

_____

Had you ever thought about all those fabulous things before?

_____

When you only think about things you don't like about yourself, how do you feel inside?

_____

_____

_____

Why is it a good idea to remember all the good things about yourself?

_____

_____

_____

To help you remember the great things about yourself, color the message below.

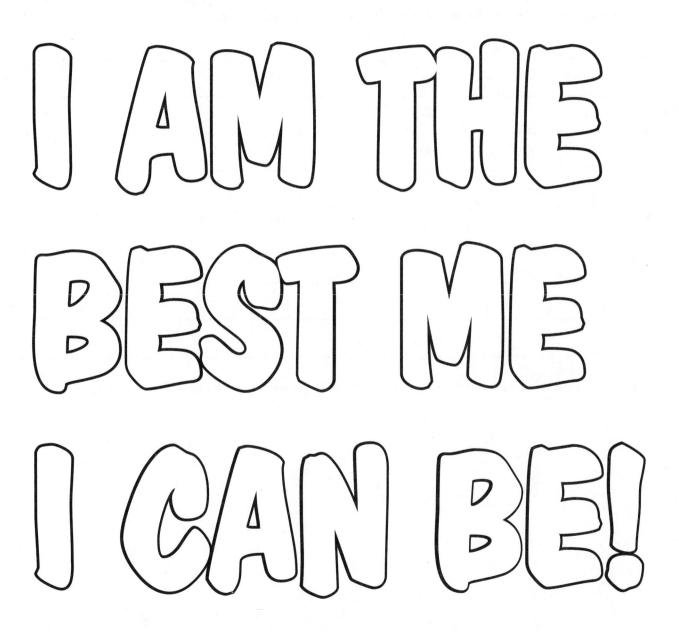

I AM THE BEST ME I CAN BE!

Sometimes, grown-ups use words they don't explain to kids.

Here are two words you may have heard lately and wondered about: "sexual abuse." On the lines below, write what you think these words mean.

_____

_____

_____

_____

_____

_____

_____

_____

Words can be confusing, so let's make sure you know what these words mean.

"Sexual abuse" is when a grown-up or older kid touches your private parts or makes you touch their private parts. It can also mean someone showing you their private parts or making you show them your private parts. It is also called "secret touching" because it usually happens without other people knowing. The other person may have told you to keep it a secret, or you may have been afraid to tell. Remember, it is NEVER a good idea to keep sexual abuse or secret touching a secret.

Do you have any questions? Write them here, and your counselor can help you answer them.

1. _____

2. _____

3. _____

4. _____

5. _____

Calico the Cat

Once upon a time, in a faraway land lived a cat named Calico. She was very beautiful and she was dearly loved by her family. Usually, she felt very good about herself and expected good things to happen. All of those good feelings suddenly changed one day, when she went walking in the flower garden and was attacked by sneaky, mean Willie the Weasel.

"You're nothing but a stupid fur ball," yelled Willie, giving one more shove before he darted away.

The way Willie grabbed her and the mean words he said hurt Calico a lot. When she got home, she was deeply shaken. Her mother could tell she was feeling scared and sad, and maybe something else. Try as she did, Calico had a hard time telling Mother Cat what happened. When the story finally came out, Mother Cat knew she had to do something to help. So she rushed Calico over to see Olivia the Owl, who was wise and would know what to do.

"I'll never be happy again for the rest of my life," wailed Calico as she finished her story about Willie.

"Certainly you will, my dear. It will just take time and some practice with your thoughts," advised Olivia.

At first, Calico did not know what Olivia meant. They visited several times, talking about important ways to help young cats feel okay. Calico was surprised to learn that many of her feelings came from what she thought about, not just from what had happened to her.

"I didn't know that!" said Calico.

"Few people do," said Olivia, "but it is an important lesson to learn so you can help your feelings heal."

Sometimes, Olivia had Calico practice saying happier thoughts in front of a mirror so she could see and hear the message as well as thinking it. "I am capable, lovable, and worthwhile," she repeated to herself, just as Olivia had taught her. Gradually, she could feel a difference taking place inside her, and she found herself smiling, playing, and laughing more, just as she used to do.

The day came when Calico felt just fine again, and she knew that her feelings had healed. Of course, she was a little smarter than before, because she understood many new things. Willie also apologized in a letter, and he was not allowed to wander around by himself without a grown-up watching him closely every minute. Calico accepted his apology but was always careful around him, which was the right thing to do. After all, he was still a weasel!

Months and years passed, and Calico grew to be a fine adult cat. She became an expert in helping other cats feel better again when they had had bad things happen to them.

"What is the most important thing for me to learn?" asked one cat.

"Remember that your thoughts cause your feelings," said Calico. "You can make yourself feel better by practicing new and better thoughts."

Not bad advice for cats, and it was pretty good advice for people, too!

For this activity, you can use a real hula hoop or an imaginary one. Put your hoop over your head and then hold it at waist level. If you are using an imaginary hoop, picture it pressed against your back and sticking out about two feet in front of you. Now, think of the space inside the hoop as your own personal space or Magic Circle. It's about two or three feet around you. This space belongs to you, and only you can decide if it is okay for someone else to come inside that space.

Try this with a friend:

Face each other from across the room. Stay still, while your friend walks very slowly toward you. When your friend gets about two or three feet away, you will probably start to feel uncomfortable. You may find it is difficult to keep looking your friend in the eyes, and you may feel a little embarrassed. Do you know why? Because your friend has come into your Magic Circle.

Put the hula hoop around you again. You'll notice that your body is probably not right in the center of the hoop. Most people hold hoops against their backs and sides, with a much bigger circle in front. A Magic Circle, or personal space, is like that too—people usually need the most space in front of them and less space in the back or on the sides.

Now, try this with a friend:

Start out across the room from each other, but sideways. Stay still, while your friend comes toward you with small sidesteps. When you start to feel uncomfortable, you'll know that your friend has reached the edge of your Magic Circle. Notice how close you are to each other. Most people find they don't need as much personal space from the side as they do in the front.

Each person's Magic Circle is a different size, so people may step into each other's personal space without realizing it. If someone walks up to you, and it feels uncomfortably close, you have a right to step back and say you need a little more room. But, how would you know if you were inside someone else's Magic Circle, if the other person doesn't tell you? Some people won't look directly at you if you are in their personal space; others may just look uncomfortable. Try backing away a little bit and see if that helps. Remember, everyone has the right to have their Magic Circles respected.

Can you answer these questions about Magic Circles?

1. The size of most people's Magic Circles is about equal to the space inside a hula hoop.

    True   False

2. When someone is inside your Magic Circle without your permission, you can tell they are too close because you feel happy and calm.

    True   False

3. Most people need more space on the sides of their Magic Circle than they do in front.

    True   False

4. If someone is inside your Magic Circle without your permission, you can ask them to back up or you can back up a little.

    True   False

5. Only your Magic Circle counts. It's okay for you to stand very close to other people and ignore their Magic Circles.

    True   False

There are three kinds of touches: good, bad, and secret. Sometimes, it can be confusing to figure out what kind of touch is happening. Good touches are usually ones you like, and they make you feel good. Bad touches are ones that hurt, like biting, kicking, and hitting, and you should always tell a grown-up who can help you about them. Secret touches are when someone touches your private parts or wants you to touch their private parts. Always tell a grown-up you trust right away if you get a secret touch, even if it is scary and hard to talk about.

Draw a line from each example to the kind of touch it is.

EXAMPLE	TOUCH

Your friend gives you a high-five.

A boy at school hits you in the back.

GOOD

Someone you know shakes your hand.

A person you don't like kisses you.

You get an email about touching private parts.

Dad gives you a hug when he gets home.

You are asked to touch someone's private parts.

BAD

A boy pulls your hair really hard.

Your little brother bites your leg.

A friend of your family comes in while you are taking a bath and won't leave when you ask him to.

A girl tells you she's going to beat you up.

A man touches your private parts and says you shouldn't tell anyone.

SECRET

Your aunt pats you on your bottom in front of your parents, and you don't like it.

Your brother taps you on the head and then starts tapping so hard that it hurts.

The lady next door pats your head when she gives you cookies.

Some touches feel good, some feel bad, some hurt, some make you smile, and some make you feel creepy-crawly inside. Some touches are fun to talk about. Some are scary to talk about, and maybe someone even said you weren't supposed to talk about them.

Let's talk some more about the three kinds of touches:

GOOD   BAD   SECRET

Good Touches

Good touches are ones you like, and they make you feel good inside.

What are some examples of good touches?

_____

_____

Circle all the words that tell how someone who gets a good touch might feel.

HAPPY   WORRIED   SCARED   EXCITED   CONFUSED   SURPRISED

PROUD   HURT   EMBARRASSED   UPSET   MAD   SAD   SORRY

What are your favorite good touches to get?

_____

_____

What are your favorite good touches to give?

_____

_____

What can you do if someone wants to give you a good touch, but you don't want it, like if your grandma hugs you too tightly?

_____

_____

_____

Bad Touches

Bad touches are ones that hurt; they do not make you feel good inside.

What are some examples of bad touches?

_____

_____

Circle all the words that tell how someone who gets a bad touch might feel.

HAPPY   WORRIED   SCARED   EXCITED   CONFUSED   SURPRISED

PROUD   HURT   EMBARRASSED   UPSET   MAD   SAD   SORRY

What are your least favorite touches to get?

_____

_____

What are some bad touches you have gotten?

_____

Is it okay for someone to give you a bad touch?

_____

What should you do if someone gives you a bad touch?

_____

What can you do if you need help, but you feel scared about asking for it?

_____

Secret Touches

Secret touches are when someone older or bigger than you touches your private parts or wants you to touch their private parts.

What is a secret touch?

_____

_____

Circle all the words that tell how someone who gets a secret touch might feel.

HAPPY   WORRIED   SCARED   EXCITED   CONFUSED   SURPRISED

PROUD   HURT   EMBARRASSED   UPSET   MAD   SAD   SORRY

What should someone do if they get a secret touch?

_____

_____

Even if you feel scared, can you still talk about a secret touch you got? What can you do?

_____

_____

_____

_____

Lots of touches are very good, but there are some touches you may not like at all. Sometimes, touches start out one way and then they change. Sometimes, touches can give you mixed-up feelings inside.

For each story below, tell what you think about what happened.

Mary and her brother were playing tag in the yard. They were having fun and laughing. When Mary tagged her brother before he could tag her, he would get mad. After that, he would hit Mary very hard every time he tagged her. The game stopped being fun. What happened? What could Mary do?

_____

_____

_____

_____

Jody's uncle loves to hear her laugh. Jody's toes are very ticklish, and her uncle sometimes tickles her feet. It is fun and Jody laughs. Sometimes, he holds her legs and tickles her feet too long. She laughs so much it's hard to breathe, and she feels scared. How did the good touching change? What should Jody do?

_____

_____

_____

_____

Simon is scared to walk home. A boy who lives on his street thinks its funny to push kids onto the sidewalk. Twice this week, Simon has been pushed down. What are some ideas that might help Simon with this problem?

_____

_____

_____

_____

Lisa really likes her babysitter Susan. Susan asks Lisa to take off her clothes and pretend she's a fashion model. Lisa is embarrassed, but she doesn't want Susan to be mad and stop liking her. Lisa also wants to be a model, so she does what Susan asks. Susan takes pictures and tells Lisa not to tell her parents, because she wants to surprise them with the pictures later. Lisa feels funny inside, and Susan never shows the pictures to her parents. What kind of touch is this? Was it okay for Susan to tell Lisa to do this? What can Lisa do?

_____

_____

_____

_____

Maybe you wish you had been bigger and stronger when the secret touching happened so that you could have stopped it from happening. But grown-ups are bigger than kids, and big kids are bigger than little kids—and you weren't bigger and stronger. Even when you get older, it's important to remember that you were little when it happened.

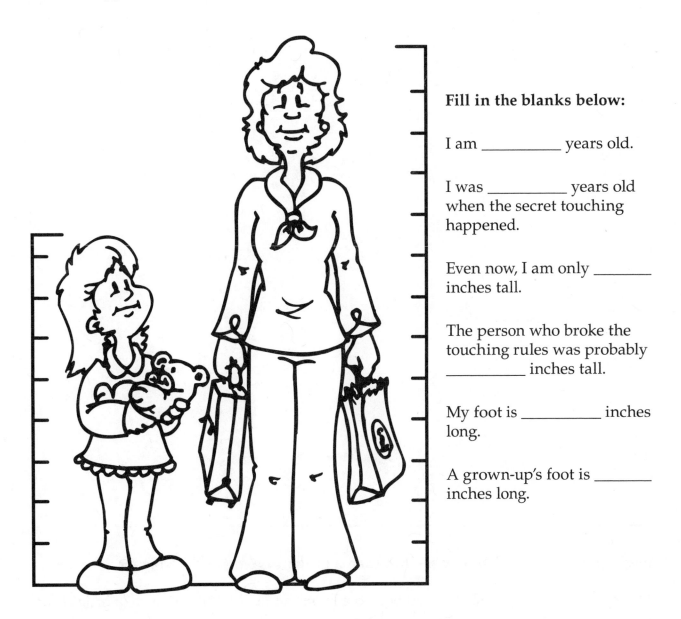

Fill in the blanks below:

I am _____ years old.

I was _____ years old when the secret touching happened.

Even now, I am only _____ inches tall.

The person who broke the touching rules was probably _____ inches tall.

My foot is _____ inches long.

A grown-up's foot is _____ inches long.

In the space below, trace your hand in one color. Then trace your counselor's hand in another color. See which one is bigger.

Right now, are you bigger or smaller than a grown-up?   Bigger   Smaller

Remember, you may wish you had been big enough to fight, but you were a little child.

Priscilla the Problem Solver

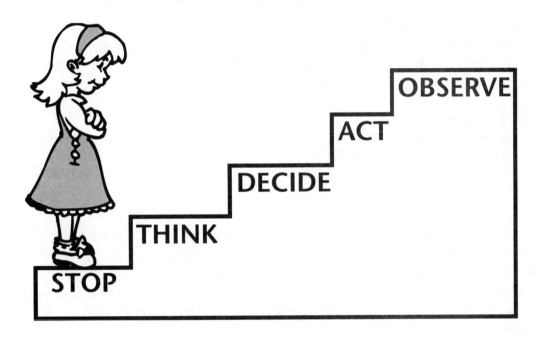

Once there was a girl named Priscilla. When she was little, Priscilla was very, very active. She stayed busy all day long, playing one thing and then another. Her mother wondered where she got all her energy. Sometimes, Priscilla would see something interesting and just grab it, without thinking first. One day, the most interesting thing around was the cat's tail, so Priscilla grabbed it. Whaack! The cat scratched Priscilla's hand with his sharp claws.

"Ouch!" Priscilla yelped.

Another time, Priscilla got interested in her mother's fine tea set. Crrraaaash!

"Oh, no," said Mother. "Why did you grab my tea set, Priscilla?"

And so Priscilla had more accidents and scrapes than most kids, until she started to get a little older. Then, when Priscilla was in the third grade, a special guest came to speak to her class about problem solving. He said that it was a good idea to practice the steps of problem solving all the time so they would get to be habits. Priscilla learned that problem solving involves following these steps just the right way:

Step One – STOP
Step Two – THINK
Step Three – DECIDE
Step Four – ACT
Step Five – OBSERVE

Priscilla practiced and practiced. She practiced on Mondays and she practiced on fun days. She practiced in the morning and she practiced at night. She practiced until she got everything right. In a few weeks, Priscilla noticed something had changed in her life. She didn't have nearly as many accidents. And she rarely did things that made people mad.

Oh, she wasn't perfect, and she still made some mistakes. But everyone makes a few mistakes, so that was okay. She just used the mistakes to learn what to do better next time. Soon, life was much smoother for Priscilla. As time went by, Priscilla grew up to be a fine young woman that nearly everyone liked.

Guess what Priscilla did with all her problem-solving skills? She became famous for giving advice in the newspaper. Thousands of people read her newspaper column and listened carefully to her advice. And Priscilla's advice was very, very good because she used her problem-solving skills. She would think about everything possible that might be done and then pick the best choice to recommend.

Sometimes, Priscilla needed more ideas than she had in her own head, and that was okay. She just asked her friends for ideas. Sometimes, she even needed special ideas from scientists and engineers, sometimes from doctors and lawyers, and sometimes from pilots and sailors. As she tried to solve problems, Priscilla met more and more new people. That was good! She loved to talk to people and ask them about their ideas. It was fun, and she learned so much from others.

Perhaps the most exciting thing that happened to Priscilla is that she even got a special award from the president for being so helpful to so many people. It said:

To Priscilla the Problem Solver—A True National Treasure

And she really was a treasure!

What might happen if you practiced problem-solving skills as much as Priscilla did?

_____

_____

_____

_____

In the space below, draw a picture of something you might be doing really well a year from now, if you practiced problem-solving skills a lot.

Write about what your picture shows:

_____

_____

_____

_____

_____

Think of something you do a lot that is a problem; which problem-solving skills could help? Draw a picture of it here.

Write about what your picture shows:

_____

_____

_____

_____

_____

Priscilla the Problem Solver

Imagine yourself as a grown-up who has great problem-solving skills. Draw a picture of what you might do to use your skills.

Write about what your picture shows:

Larry the Lobster

Once upon a time there was a lobster named Larry. He lived in the ocean. When Larry was a little lobster, he had many rough times. Once a big fish nearly ate him! Another time, a huge storm tossed him around in the waves. Sometimes even when he had really good times playing in the water and chasing bubbles he kept on thinking about the things that went wrong and the things he did not like about himself instead of all the good things that were around him and inside him. Poor Larry—he was sad, a lot, but he kept on keeping on the best he could. Larry went to Ocean School and tried to make friends with Cody the Cod Fish, Ollie the Octopus, and Sally the Star Fish. Because he was so sad about so many things, it was hard for him to remember what an outstanding young lobster he really was. In fact, he thought there might be something wrong with him, because he was hard and bumpy and had no suction cups or tentacles to help him move around like Sally the Star Fish and did not have smooth soft skin like Cody the Cod Fish or lots of long arms like Ollie the Octopus so he could not reach out and hold eight things at one time. He was not just like his friends.

"Why can't I be just like my friends," Larry sighed. Cody, Ollie, and Sally tried to reassure him, but after a while they got tired of Larry being so grumpy and grouchy and ALWAYS saying bad things about himself. Cody, Ollie, and Sally were all really nice ocean creatures, but when they hung around Larry, they started to feel sad and grumpy too. They did not like the way that felt so they tried not to hang around Larry very much. For Larry this meant more time alone and no friends.

Then one day, his teacher got worried about Larry. He didn't try hard at school, and he never answered any questions even though the teacher knew Larry was smart and knew the answers. Sometimes Larry didn't even turn in his homework and he hardly ever talked to his friends. So his teacher had an idea and sent Larry to talk to King Poseidon about his problem of not liking himself.

"I can't like myself," Larry claimed. "I am just not at all like my friends, and that is bad … isn't it?"

"Nonsense!" said King Poseidon. "You are a fine young lobster. You're not supposed to be just like everyone else. Don't you know that you are supposed to be yourself?"

"No, I didn't know that," said Larry in amazement. "I work so hard to be like my friends, but that just doesn't seem to work."

"Well, of course it doesn't work," said King Poseidon. "You aren't a codfish or an octopus or a star fish. You are a lobster and a rather fine specimen of a lobster, if I do say so. You are meant to be just who you are, Larry the Lobster, with all your special abilities and unique look. If you start telling yourself the right things instead of all the wrong things about yourself, you can learn to like yourself, just like you are. Now hold up your right claw and repeat after me. … 'I am exactly how I was meant to be. I am going to think positive things and always remember I'm special and likeable and I am a fabulous lobster.' "

Larry raised his claw and stood as tall as a lobster can stand, and even standing that way made him feel proud. He repeated what King Poseidon had said.

"Now, go on back to school and practice saying this to yourself every day," said King Poseidon. "You can use your thinking to help yourself remember how special you are. Every day when you are playing with your friends, I want you to remember the word 'PLAY'."

"PLAY" thought Larry; I know that word really well, but what can that do to help me think good things about myself?

King Poseidon explained that Larry could use the word "PLAY" to remember by using these letters:

P—is for positive thoughts. Think good thoughts, which help you remember you are great.

L—is for likeable. If you like yourself, others will like you too, so remember you are likeable.

A—is for always remembering how great you are because there is no one just like you.

Y—stands for YOU ARE FABULOUS!

"I can do it, King Poseidon, " Larry said. "I know I can do it."

"I knew it all the time, Larry," King Poseidon said as he smiled the biggest smile Larry had ever seen.

Larry did exactly that. Every time he went to PLAY with his friends or PLAY his favorite video, he recalled positive thoughts, being likeable, and always remembering that he was fabulous. By the end of the school term, he was voted class president because every one of the ocean creatures could see that Larry had really changed. The poor little lobster that used to mumble negative things about himself all the time and hold his head down in sadness didn't even look the same—no sir! When he walked down the hall of Ocean School, he held his head up high and waved his fabulous claws to all his friends as he walked by.

Sometimes it is really good to have an easy way to help us remember things.

Let's use King Poseidon's ideas for you.

Every time you PLAY a game or PLAY outside or PLAY a video or DVD or PLAY soccer, remember what PLAY stands for:

P **is for positive thoughts.**

L **is for likeable.**

A **is for always remembering you are a great kid.**

Y **stands for YOU ARE FABULOUS!**

THINK ABOUT IT

P is for positive thoughts.

What are some positive thoughts you can say to yourself or say in your head EVERY DAY to help you remember how great you are?

Here are few and you think of more.

I try really hard to do my best.

I can be a good friend.

I can ask for help when I need it.

_____

_____

_____

L is for likeable. If you learn to like yourself, it helps other people learn to like you too. It also makes it easier to make friends.

What are some things your friends like about you?

_____

_____

_____

A is for always remembering you are a great kid. There are so many great things about you.

See how many of them you can think of.

_____

_____

_____

_____

_____

_____

Y stands for "YOU ARE FABULOUS." See if you can try this. Stand up and hold your head up high and say, "I AM FABULOUS."

If you think of new things later, you can add them to your list.

Hooray for you!

My Problem-Solving Plan   Activity 19

A problem is something to be worked out or something that causes difficulty, and there are many different kinds of problems. There are everyday problems, like unexpected things that happen. Some ways of solving those problems work very well and some ways do NOT work so well. Imagine that some fruit juice got spilled onto your seat at school. If you just go ahead and sit in the chair, guess where that fruit juice is going to end up? That's right—as a big wet spot on your clothes. If you shout, "Eeew, gross! My seat's wet!" you might disrupt the class or upset the teacher. But if you quietly get a paper towel and wipe off the seat, no one is disturbed and you don't end up with wet clothes. Do you see how what you do about a problem makes a difference?

"MY PLAN"

Other kinds of problems can be more personal. What if a friend tells you that she is going to run away because she doesn't like her new stepparent? Should you keep that a secret? Should you just give her advice and then forget about it? Should you tell an adult? Should you tell your friend she can stay at your house? What you decide to do can make a big difference, can't it?

Activity 19

My Problem-Solving Plan

You can learn to solve problems well by learning and practicing these steps:

STOP

 The first step is very important. It is a reminder NOT to do anything before thinking it through. If you immediately do the first thing you think of, you will have thought about only one solution, without considering other possibilities. So the best thing to do when you recognize a problem exists is to STOP; don't do anything immediately.

THINK

The second step involves trying to imagine all the possible solutions you can think of. Including as many choices as you can come up with—even ones that are probably bad ideas—will help you stretch your imagination. If you need an answer soon, it is up to you to imagine as many possibilities as you can. If you have some time before you respond, you could ask other people for their suggestions as well.

DECIDE

The third step involves imagining how each possible solution would probably work out in real life and then making the best choice.

ACT

The fourth step involves putting the decision into action.

OBSERVE

The final step is to pay attention to the way things ACTUALLY worked out. Be like a scientist carefully watching how an experiment works out. Was it like you imagined it would be? Was it different? Did you notice other possible choices you hadn't even thought of? Remember these possibilities in case you face that same kind of problem in the future.

Let's practice these five steps on two imaginary problems. At the end of this activity, you'll find a form you can copy to use on real problems.

Problem 1

Juan was in class and there was a knock on the classroom door. Juan's teacher, Mrs. Hunnicutt, went to see who it was and stepped out into the hall to talk to another teacher for a minute. Juan's friend, Kelvin, slipped up to Mrs. Hunnicutt's desk and opened a drawer. He took something from the drawer, put it in his pocket, and went back to his seat.

STOP

The first thing Juan should do is to _____ so that he can follow the other problem-solving steps in the right order.

THINK

Juan tries to think of all the possible things he can do. Here are two choices. On the blank lines, write three more choices Juan can make.

1. Juan could yell, "Stop, thief!"

2. Juan could stay out of it completely. Mrs. Hunnicutt sometimes tells the class not to tell on each other. Maybe he should just stay quiet.

3. _____

4. _____

5. _____

DECIDE

Think about how each possible action would probably turn out. Which choice do you think Juan should make and why?

_____

_____

ACT

Juan puts his decision into action after considering everything he can think of.

OBSERVE

Since imagination can be different from what actually happens, Juan pays attention to how the situation REALLY turns out. That helps Juan decide how to handle similar situations, if they happen.

Problem 2

Shamika and Whitney are best friends. Both girls are in the fourth grade. One Monday, Whitney comes to school looking upset. She says she has a secret that Shamika must promise never to tell anyone else. Without waiting, Whitney shares that her 18-year-old cousin Terrell was visiting all the way from Kansas for the weekend. Whitney said he was a lot of fun to be with, and she didn't mind letting him use her bedroom while she slept on the sofa. In the middle of the night, Whitney woke up because Terrell was sitting on the sofa next to her, touching her underneath her nightgown. He told her not to tell so he wouldn't get in trouble, and he said that he had always thought she was very pretty. With tears in her eyes, Whitney reminds Shamika that she must not tell anybody else about this terrible secret. Today, Terrell is on his way home.

STOP

What is the first thing Shamika should do?

_____

_____

_____

THINK

What are three possible things Shamika can do?

1. _____

2. _____

3. _____

DECIDE

Write how you think each possibility would turn out. Put a star next to the one you think Shamika should choose.

1. _____

2. _____

3. _____

ACT

Shamika decides to pick your top choice and does it.

OBSERVE

The next day, Whitney tells Shamika that this is the third time Terrell has touched her inappropriately. Each time, he had promised he wouldn't do it again.

Does this information change what you think Shamika should have done?

                                                            Yes   No

Why?

_____

_____

_____

_____

_____

My problem is:

_____

_____

_____

_____

The first thing I will do is **STOP!**

Here are some possible solutions I can **THINK** of:

1. _____

2. _____

3. _____

After I have thought about how each solution might turn out, I am ready to **DECIDE**.

1. _____

2. _____

3. _____

Now, I am ready to **ACT**.

Here is what I **OBSERVE** about my solution:

_____

_____

_____

Activity 20   My Lips Are Not Sealed

You may think that keeping quiet about what happened will help you forget. Some kids' families think they shouldn't talk about things either. And some people who hurt kids or break the rules about touching may tell kids not to talk about it. But when you seal your lips and keep your feelings inside, it makes it hard for you to figure out your problems. It makes it hard for helpers to help you. It is always a better idea to talk about your feelings (good ones and bad ones too!), your problems, and your worries.

So what should you do with good things, good feelings, mixed-up feelings, problems, worries, bad things that happen, or things you don't understand? Talk about them!

Think about some things you find really hard to talk about, and write those things on the lines next to the sealed lips. If it is hard for you to think of things, try imagining what other kids may feel mixed up or worried about and that may help you remember.

_____

_____

_____

_____

_____

How would it feel to keep all those things inside and not have anyone to help you figure it out?

_____

_____

_____

Now, think of the ways that talking about what happened can help you feel better inside. On the lines next to the open lips, write how talking can make you feel better.

_____

_____

_____

_____

_____

It's important to think about who you can talk to when you have mixed-up feelings, problems, or worries. Here are some people who are usually great to talk to:

- ☐ People who love you

- ☐ People who help kids with their problems

- ☐ Your favorite teacher

- ☐ Your teachers at church or synagogue

Name some people you can talk to.

1. _____

2. _____

3. _____

4. _____

5. _____

Remember, the best way to handle mixed-up feelings, problems, or worries is to …

TALK ABOUT THEM!

Practice will make you better at just about anything you try to learn, whether it is soccer, spelling, or singing. Practice is really important for what you are learning in therapy, too. Here are some thoughts you can practice over and over again. Say them out loud as often as you can.

I should always tell a grown-up I trust about bad secrets.

I am capable, lovable, and worthwhile.

Talking about problems may not always be fun, but it can prevent bigger problems later on.

It is better to face a problem and try to solve it than to avoid it.

I can help keep myself safer by paying attention to my senses.

When someone offers me an idea I don't agree with I can store it away to think about it at some future time instead of arguing with them.

I can be better friends with someone if we practice what we both like to do together.

Telling someone who really listens all about my feelings usually makes me feel better.

I can learn to be more responsible by taking good care of myself.

I can get better and better at solving problems by learning to STOP, THINK, DECIDE, ACT, and OBSERVE.

Activity 22 All My Feelings Help Me

Some people think of feelings as being good or bad. Some call them positive or negative. A good way to think about feelings is that some feelings are COMFORTABLE and some feelings are UNCOMFORTABLE.

Excited

Frustrated

Sad

Scared

Worried

"COMFORTABLE" means something feels good, like your favorite T-shirt or a cold drink after a long day of playing.

Look at the feelings above and write down all the feelings that are COMFORTABLE for you.

_____

_____

_____

"UNCOMFORTABLE" means something doesn't feel good, like a pair of shoes that is too tight or the itchy feeling from that sweater your grandmother gave you. Those feelings may make you feel bad inside or you might not understand them.

What feelings are UNCOMFORTABLE for you?

_____

_____

_____

All feelings matter—even the ones you don't like to feel. They give you important information, like finding pieces to a puzzle. To finish a puzzle, you need all the pieces, not just a favorite few.

From the feelings you just listed, choose four comfortable feelings and four uncomfortable feelings. Write them below and then answer the questions about them.

Comfortable Feelings	*Why I Like That Feeling*	*How Can That Feeling Help Me?*

Uncomfortable Feelings	*Why I Don't Like That Feeling*	*How Can That Feeling Help Me?*

Activity 23 The Creepy Crawlies

Have you ever felt a hair on your arm but not been able to see it? Did you ever get the feeling that someone was behind you and turned around to see your neighbor's dog right there? That happens because your brain pays attention to things you may not notice. It's the way your brain helps you know what is going on around you, even when you are concentrating on something else, like doing homework or trying to draw a really good picture.

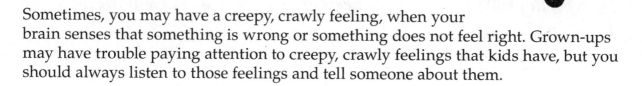

Sometimes, you may have a creepy, crawly feeling, when your brain senses that something is wrong or something does not feel right. Grown-ups may have trouble paying attention to creepy, crawly feelings that kids have, but you should always listen to those feelings and tell someone about them.

Can you ever remember having a creepy, crawly feeling?

Yes   No

How do you know you are having a creepy, crawly feeling? What does it feel like inside?

_____

_____

_____

Did you ever have a creepy, crawly feeling about the person who touched you in the wrong way?

Yes   No

If you did, what was that feeling like inside?

_____

_____

_____

Did you ever try to tell anyone about that creepy, crawly feeling?

Yes   No

If you did, what happened?

_____

_____

_____

If you did have a creepy, crawly feeling about the person who touched you, does that mean you could have stopped the touching?

Yes   No

If you didn't have a creepy, crawly feeling about the person who touched you, does that mean the touching was your fault?

Yes   No

Who can you talk to when you are having a creepy, crawly feeling?

_____

_____

_____

Should you keep a creepy, crawly feeling to yourself?

Yes   No

What should you do if the first grown-up you tell doesn't listen?

_____

_____

_____

If you had a creepy, crawly feeling and it turned out that nothing was wrong, should you ignore the next creepy, crawly feeling you have?

Yes   No

Why?

_____

_____

_____

Can a creepy, crawly feeling be a good thing?

Yes   No

Why?

_____

_____

_____

Did you know that thoughts can get stuck in your brain? When something gets stuck in your brain, it is very hard for you to stop thinking about it; it comes up in your brain over and over again. Thoughts that get stuck can be good things, like if your parents tell you that in a few weeks you are going to Disney World. You'd think about it all the time, and it would be a POSITIVE THOUGHT for your brain to have. But sometimes what gets stuck in your brain is not so great. What if a friend said something mean about you? What if you kept thinking bad things about yourself, like that you should have known something bad was going to happen, or even that what happened was your fault? Those things are WRONG and they are called NEGATIVE THOUGHTS. It is hard when negative thoughts get stuck in your brain.

Using a color you don't like, write the negative thoughts that get stuck in your brain on the lines to the left. You can add more lines if you need to. Next, think about how these thoughts make you feel. On the lines next to your negative thoughts, write your feelings.

Negative Thoughts

_____

_____

_____

_____

_____

_____

_____

_____

_____

_____

Negative Feelings

_____

_____

_____

_____

_____

_____

_____

_____

_____

_____

Using a color you do like, write the positive thoughts that are stuck in your brain. Again, add more lines if you need to. Think about how these positive thoughts make you feel, and write those feelings beside your positive thoughts.

Positive Thoughts

_____

_____

_____

_____

_____

_____

_____

_____

Positive Feelings

_____

_____

_____

_____

_____

_____

_____

_____

Negative thoughts make it hard for you to do your best. What positive thoughts can you think of to replace the negative thoughts that are stuck in your brain?

_____

_____

_____

_____

Positive thoughts help you do your best and feel good inside. How can you help good thoughts get stuck in your brain?

_____

_____

_____

_____

Have you ever read the book called *The Little Engine That Could*? If you have never read it, try to check it out at the library or get a grown-up you know to help you find it. In the story, the Little Engine had a big job to do. He had to figure out how to get all the train cars over a HUGE hill. It was very hard to do, and the Little Engine did not think he could pull all those cars. Guess what happened? With help, the Little Engine did it!

Do you know what the helper told the Little Engine? He told the little train to BELIEVE he could do it and to try hard. He told the Little Engine to use his mouth and his brain to help him. How could the Little Engine's brain and mouth help him pull all those train cars? By thinking positively—the Little Engine kept saying, "I think I can, I think I can" as he was trying so hard to pull those heavy train cars—and he could!

The next time you are trying to figure something out or have something really hard to do, tell yourself:

I THINK I CAN, I THINK I CAN.

I Think I Can

Is there something really hard you have been trying to do or trying to figure out? Coming to counseling and talking about mixed-up feelings, problems, and worries can be really hard. Talking about secret touching and what has happened can be really hard, too. Is there anything you have wanted to do and think you can't? What might have happened if the Little Engine had kept saying, "I think I can't, I think I can't?"

What are some of the things you tell yourself that DON'T help you do your best?

1. _____

2. _____

3. _____

4. _____

5. _____

What could you tell yourself that would help you?

1. _____

2. _____

3. _____

4. _____

5. _____

Activity 26

Taking Good Care of Teddy

Do you have a favorite teddy bear or a stuffed animal? Did you know that stuffed animals and dolls are very important in helping you learn how to take care of things? By learning how to take care of stuffed animals, you are learning how to be a good parent later on. Learning to take care of others also helps you like yourself more, because you will realize how important you are.

Think about a stuffed animal that is special to you. It might be a teddy bear, a stuffed rabbit, or even a doll. Let's call it "Teddy." Now, think about all of the things you can do to take good care of Teddy.

Finding Sunshine After the Storm

Here are some ideas. You can:

☐ Keep him warm on a cool day by covering him with your blanket.

☐ Show that you love him by rubbing his fur gently, the way you would like to be stroked.

☐ Pretend to feed him small amounts of food.

☐ Share special things with him, like your favorite book.

☐ Talk to him in ways that help him feel loved.

What else can you do to take good care of Teddy?

1. _____

2. _____

3. _____

4. _____

5. _____

If Teddy could talk to you, what do you think he would tell you?

_____

_____

_____

_____

If Teddy could talk to his friends, what would he say are the best things about the way you take care of him?

_____

_____

_____

_____

Teddy is lucky he has you!

Prickly Pete

Once upon a time, a little porcupine named Pete was trying hard to figure out how porcupine quills worked. Pete worried, because try as he might, he could not get his quills to stand up or shoot out like the big porcupines could. What would he do when he needed them to help him be safe? Pete spent all his time worrying that something would happen and his quills would not work. He had no time for friends and no time for fun. Even at night, Pete dreamed about all the things that might happen and how he would not be ready for them.

One day, while his friends Rupert Rabbit, Frannie Fox, and Harry Hedgehog were playing tag, Pete stood on the side, looking at his quills and wondering what to do. He was not even watching his friends as they had fun playing in the forest.

"Come on and play," said Frannie Fox.

"Yeah you never play anymore," added Rupert Rabbit.

They all gathered around urging Pete to just have fun and stop worrying about his quills so much.

"I can't play. I have to get ready for shooting my quills, and they aren't working," Pete said in a very loud voice.

"Well, maybe you could play anyway," said Harry Hedgehog.

"No, I can't. Now go away," Pete answered, as he kept looking at his quills.

All of a sudden, out shot Pete's quills, hitting his friends as they howled with pain!

"What did you do that for?" yelped Frannie. "We were leaving you alone like you wanted."

"Ouch, ouch, ouch," cried Rupert and Harry.

Pete could not believe it. His quills had worked, but they had hurt his friends. Suddenly, Pete's quills shot out again, before he could stop them. Rupert ducked, Frannie dodged, and Harry Hedgehog dug in the dirt to avoid getting hurt again. The animal friends ran off, yelping with pain and mad at how Pete had acted.

For days, no one went near Pete for fear he would shoot out his quills and hurt them. But Pete was so afraid his quills would stop working that, sometimes, he just let them shoot out wherever they wanted to, even though it meant no one wanted to be around him. Pete seemed to think that keeping his friends away was okay, as long as he could defend himself if he were scared.

Several days went by, and Pete was out in the woods alone when he met a kindly cougar named Cody, who was sunning himself on a branch of a pine tree.

"What are you doing out here by yourself, little one?" Cody Cougar asked.

The porcupine looked up, and he felt a little bit scared.

"No one wants to be around me, 'cause my quills keep flying out and hurting them," said Pete.

"Why are you shooting your quills out at your friends? Did they hurt you or something?" asked Cody, licking his paws.

"No, but at first, I couldn't get my quills to work right. They just came out by themselves. Now, I want them to keep coming out so I will be safe," Pete answered, watching the cougar very carefully.

"Let me get this straight. You think that you have to worry all the time about keeping yourself safe and that you can't control throwing your quills out at your friends?" Cody asked, as he looked at the porcupine in disbelief.

"Yes, that's exactly right," replied Pete. "I have to be safe so sometimes my quills just come out."

"Well, you have a lot to learn about being safe and about friends," said Cody, as he climbed down from the tree.

"I know plenty," Pete said in a loud voice, trying to sound strong and brave.

"If you know so much, where are your friends," Cody responded with a smirk, "and what are you doing out here alone talking to a cougar?"

Pete had not even realized that cougars might like to eat porcupines for dinner. He had been so busy worrying about everything that he had not really paid attention to what was happening around him. Cody could see that Pete was getting upset.

"Don't worry. I'm not hungry," Cody said, "but I would like you to walk with me so we can talk for a little while."

Cody and Pete walked in the warm sun shining down through the trees. Cody was a very wise cougar, and he talked to Pete about the importance of making good choices.

"Pete, when you choose to spend all your time worrying, you miss out on all the fun," Cody explained. "Your friends and family miss out on having you around to enjoy all the things friends and families like to do."

Pete had never thought about it that way. As he kicked the dust with his paw, he looked at the cougar and said, "I never thought of that. I just didn't want to have something happen that I wasn't ready for."

The cougar shook his head. "You also didn't realize that when your mind was so busy worrying, you probably weren't noticing all the other things going on around you, " Cody said.

Pete had to agree with that, too. When he worried, he didn't think about anything else. Cody went on to explain how that meant he might miss out on clues all around him. If he were too busy worrying, Pete might even ignore his feelings, which were like clues that could help him be safe.

Next, Cody Cougar talked about choices. Pete had thought it was a good choice to let his quills fly everywhere. As much as he hated to admit it, it was not a good choice because it kept all the people that loved him away from him. It made them afraid of what he might do next.

They talked for a long time, and Pete learned many new lessons about choices, thinking, and worrying. It felt good inside to know he could make good choices, not worry, and still be safe. Pete was very glad he had met Cody. Pete thanked him for his help and ran to the place where Frannie, Rupert, and Harry were playing.

"I'm here," said Pete, "and wait until I tell you all the things I learned!"

With that, all his friends gathered around and they talked and laughed as Pete shared the lessons he had learned.

Are You Like a Porcupine?   Activity 28

If you read the Prickly Pete story, you've already learned some things about porcupines. Let's see what you've learned.

How do porcupines keep themselves safe?

_____

_____

Even though porcupines are very small, very few bigger animals bother them. Do you know why?

_____

_____

Those pointy, prickly things all over porcupines are called "quills." Most often, porcupines use their quills wisely to protect themselves, but Prickly Pete had a BIG problem with his quills. Instead of just protecting himself, he let his quills hurt his friends. Did you know sometimes kids can act like porcupines? Just like Prickly Pete, kids may think they are keeping themselves safe when they are just getting themselves into trouble.

Do you ever act like a porcupine? Maybe you yell at people you aren't even mad at because you have too many mad feelings stuck inside. Maybe you don't talk at all because you are afraid of what you might say. You can use the porcupine below to help you share your feelings without hurting others. Think about things you do to try to be safe (like yelling or not talking at all) as being like quills. Write those things on the lines next to the porcupine.

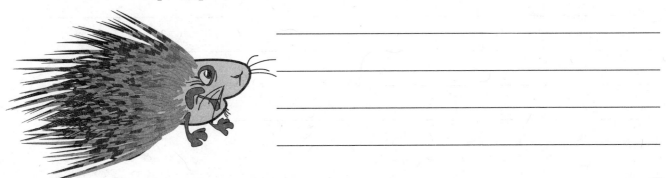

_____

_____

_____

_____

Now think about what feelings make you do those things. Maybe you yell because you are angry about what happened, or you don't talk because you are afraid you might say the wrong thing or tell more than you want to. Write your feelings on the lines below.

Then try to figure out what you can do to help yourself with your feelings. For example, if you feel sad, one thing you can do is to cry while your mom rocks you. Write your good choices on the lines next to your feelings.

Feelings	*Good Choices*
_____	_____
_____	_____
_____	_____
_____	_____
_____	_____
_____	_____
_____	_____
_____	_____
_____	_____
_____	_____

I'm Mad, I'm Mad, I'm Mad   Activity 29

Everyone gets mad sometimes. Mad feelings are okay to have but usually it just doesn't feel very good to have them. Sometimes mad feelings can feel so big inside that it is scary. It can be hard to understand them or know what to do to help deal with them. Do you have any mad feelings inside of you?

So let's think about mad feelings. "Mad" and "angry" are the same thing, so sometimes people say they are mad and sometimes they say they are angry.

Did you know that sometimes kids try to pretend that they don't get mad?

Circle the reasons you think kids might pretend they are not mad. If you can think of more, just write them in.

You aren't supposed to be mad; you are supposed to be nice.

If the mad feelings come out, you would have to hurt someone.

If you pretend you aren't mad, you won't ever have to talk about mad feelings.

The mad feelings are so big you are afraid to let them out.

It is not okay to be mad.

Pretending you are not mad makes mad feelings go away.

If you let the mad feelings come out, you will be mad all the time.

You have seen your mom or dad get mad, and that was really scary.

Now look at all the reasons you circled. How many of them are TRUE?????

8   5   3   1   0

Guess what? The answer is NONE!!!!!

Why is it good to talk about mad feelings?

Circle all the reasons that are TRUE.

Sometimes drawing a mad picture will help mad feelings get better.

If I am mad, I will have to break something.

If I get mad, it makes me a bad kid.

Talking about mad feelings makes them get worse.

My counselor needs to know the things that make me really get mad.

If I am mad about something, I can ride my bike or run and it will help me feel better.

Mad feelings help us know when something is wrong.

Talking about mad feelings helps them get better.

Let your counselor help you figure out your mad feelings—bring your homework book to counseling next time!

Remember that mad feelings are okay to have. Everyone gets mad sometimes. What are some of the things that make you REALLY mad? Not just a little mad but REALLY mad, like there's a volcano inside you ready to explode. Sometimes it's hard to think of the things and hard to write them down, but it's okay to write them down so you can help them get better.

Write the things that make you mad; write them around the volcano.

Remember that everyone gets mad sometimes and that is okay. Our mad feelings can help us. But we have to make good choices about what we do with our mad feelings because it is never okay to hurt someone, hurt an animal, or break something special because of our mad feelings. Mad feelings get worse if we keep them inside, so here are two ways you can help yourself when you feel very mad, like a volcano inside.

I can write about my angry feelings.

_____

_____

_____

_____

_____

_____

I can draw my angry feelings.

Working Off Your Anger   Activity 31

Have you ever been so angry that you couldn't sit still? Sometimes nothing will help except using up some of your energy. It's okay to feel like that, but there is a right way and a wrong way to use up all that energy.

The wrong way is to hurt a person or an animal or to mess up something of value. You have the right to your feelings, but you do NOT have a right to be destructive.

On the lines below, list ten things that would NOT be okay to do when you are angry.

1. _____

2. _____

3. _____

4. _____

5. _____

6. _____

7. _____

8. _____

9. _____

10. _____

What is okay to do? First, it might be helpful to know that when you are angry, your body gets ready for action. So what usually will help you the most is something that lets you use your muscles a lot, like playing a sport.

Here are a few ideas for activities that use up lots of energy. See if you can finish the list with your own ideas:

- ☐ Riding a bike up a hill

- ☐ Running

- ☐ Sweeping out the garage

- ☐ Doing lots of sit-ups

- ☐ Mopping the floor

- ☐ Raking the leaves in the yard

- ☐ _____

- ☐ _____

- ☐ _____

- ☐ _____

- ☐ _____

Would your mom or dad be okay with all of these activities? If not, cross out the ones they don't approve of. If you're not sure, you can ask. Now try one of these activities. See if you can keep doing the activity until you start to feel tired. That's when your body is telling you it has had enough, and you can start to relax again.

Good luck! You can do it!

Being responsible means thinking ahead about what you should do and then doing it. Kids aren't responsible for many things in their lives, like finding a place to live or earning money to buy food. But there are a lot of things you can be responsible for, and when you take responsibility, you can feel proud of yourself.

Read the list below and put a check next to all the things you will be responsible for. At the end of the list, add your own ideas.

Starting today, I am going to be responsible for:

☐ Checking the weather report and picking the right clothes for the weather

☐ Brushing my teeth at least twice every day

☐ Doing my homework without being told

☐ Taking a bath or shower every day without being told

☐ Doing my chores without reminders

☐ Combing or brushing my hair

☐ _____

☐ _____

☐ _____

☐ _____

☐ _____

I can do it!

You probably know a lot of rules about strangers, like:

- Don't talk to strangers.
- Don't get into a car with a stranger.
- Don't leave school with someone you don't know.

These are all important rules, but knowing who is a stranger can be very confusing. A stranger is someone you don't know, but not all strangers are scary, and sometimes you have to talk to them. When you go to the supermarket with your parents, you might talk to the person at the cash register even though that person is probably a stranger.

Strangers are people you don't know, but sometimes strangers can be good helpers. Those strangers are called "safe people." On the next page are some questions that can help you find safe people.

Where are some places you go every day or every week?

_____

_____

_____

What are some reasons you might need a helper at those places?

_____

_____

_____

Who are some safe people you can ask for help?

_____

_____

_____

What about these people makes them good people to ask for help?

_____

_____

_____

With your parents' permission, practice asking these people for help so if you need them, you will already know how to do it. For example, you could ask the person behind a store counter what time it is or how to find something in the store.

It can be hard to think good things about yourself, especially when something bad has happened to you. But only thinking bad things about yourself can make you forget all the great things about you. Thinking positively about yourself is very important. It is great when others think good things about you, but what is most important is when you think good things about yourself.

Use the stars below to write good things about yourself. Use one color to write things people have said to you that made you feel good. Use another color to write things you wish people would say to you. Use a third color to write good things you can say to yourself.

Now remember what you have written, because all these great things are about you!

Things People Have Said to You That Made You Feel Good

Finding Sunshine After the Storm

Things You Wish People Would Say to You

Good Things You Can Say to Yourself

Activity 35 Secrets

Have you ever done anything that you kept a secret, like sneaking a cookie or getting a present for a friend and not telling what it is?

Are you supposed to keep secrets or share secrets? Write your answer below.

_____

_____

_____

_____

Did you know there are secrets that are okay to keep and secrets that are NOT okay to keep? Here are some clues to help you figure out the difference.

Okay Secrets

- Are almost always about something fun
- Make you feel excited and happy
- Are meant to be shared one day

What do you think is an okay secret to keep?

1. _____

2. _____

3. _____

4. _____

5. _____

Finding Sunshine After the Storm

Not-Okay Secrets

- Are almost always about something that is confusing or wrong
- Usually make you feel scared or nervous
- Are secrets someone wants you never to tell

What do you think is a secret that is NOT okay to keep?

1. _____

2. _____

3. _____

4. _____

5. _____

How can you tell if a secret is an OKAY secret or a NOT-OKAY secret? It can be hard to know the difference, so here is a chance to practice figuring things out like a detective.

What do you think about the following secrets? Write your answers on the lines below each secret.

Dan helps his mom bake a cake for his grandpa's birthday. The family wants to surprise Grandpa, so everyone tells Dan to keep the cake a secret. Dan sees Grandpa coming. Should he keep the secret?

_____

_____

_____

Molly tells her friend Rebecca that her uncle touches her private parts sometimes. Should Rebecca keep it a secret or help Molly tell a grown-up?

_____

_____

_____

Brad sees Luke take the teacher's ruler out of her desk. Luke tells Brad he had better keep it a secret. What should Brad do? Why?

_____

_____

_____

Sally's mom buys her brother a new bike for his birthday. Her mom says, "Sally, keep it a secret until his birthday." Is this an okay secret? Why or why not?

_____

_____

_____

David's babysitter makes him take his clothes off and sit in her lap. It makes David feel funny inside even though he likes his babysitter. She says it's their little secret. What should David do?

_____

_____

_____

Karen and Kim like to go to Miss Charlotte's house. One day, Miss Charlotte asks them to play a game where they take turns touching each other's private parts. Miss Charlotte says if people knew about their game they would be mad and jealous. Can you help Karen and Kim know what to do?

_____

_____

_____

Sarah and her best friend Jane go to the store. Jane steals candy and gives some to Sarah. On the way home, Jane tells Sarah she better not tell because she ate the candy so she would be in trouble too. What should Sarah do?

_____

_____

_____

Brian walks home from school alone and sometimes takes a short cut that he's not supposed to take. The past few days, a man has followed him every time he's taken the short cut. Brian doesn't know the man, and he's afraid he'll get in trouble for taking the short cut. Should Brian keep it a secret that a man has been following him?

_____

_____

_____

Laurie breaks her mom's coffee cup. She tries to put it back together with glue, and she puts it in the cabinet. Laurie sees Mom pouring hot coffee in the cup. What should Laurie do?

_____

_____

_____

Remember, some secrets are okay to keep and some secrets need to be shared with a trusted adult as soon as possible. If you feel confused about whether or not to share a secret, that is a big clue. What does that clue mean?

TELL A GROWN-UP YOU TRUST RIGHT AWAY!

Do you wear glasses? Many people do to correct a vision problem. Thank goodness that glasses are available! Can you imagine how difficult it was for people with vision problems BEFORE glasses were invented?! Not being able to see clearly is just one kind of perceptual handicap. Other perceptual handicaps might include things like a hearing loss or inability to taste or smell. A *handicap* is anything that puts a person at a disadvantage. *Perception* is when our brain gives some meaning to what one of our senses experiences or when our brain remembers or imagines things. Problems with perception could come from problems with one of our five senses, like a vision problem. But perception problems could also come from lots of other things like not having enough information to understand something, or faulty thinking about what we see or hear, or misuse of our imagination or memory.

All of those possible problems related to perception we could call *Perceptual Blindness*, or PB. Perhaps one of the more difficult kinds of PB is when we think we have something figured out correctly but we are mistaken. Raise your hand if you have ever been wrong about something when you thought you were right. I have my hand raised, do you? When we think about PB this way, it includes EVERYBODY sometimes. In fact, PB includes every single person on this whole planet! That makes PB a Worldwide Handicap.

Complicating the picture a little more, we may sometimes think we DO know the answer to something when we are wrong, wrong, wrong. So believing something sometimes helps, but sometimes our beliefs can be part of PB when our beliefs are off-track.

Hey, don't be sad or discouraged, this is just part of being human. We can't know everything all the time. And we can't have correct beliefs about everything we think, because that is just not possible for humans to do. The fact is that sometimes we don't have enough information to solve a problem, and sometimes what we believe is not really the way it is. That's just part of life.

What can you do about PB? You are already doing one of the things you can do. You are going to school to learn, and you are working on this activity workbook to learn even more. Good for you! We never stop learning, and working hard to learn more is an important part of dealing with PB.

But what about beliefs we have that might be wrong? Well, one of the things we can do about that is to know it happens sometimes because we are human. So when someone says they have a different belief from our own, perhaps we should listen and consider their belief carefully. Perhaps we should remind ourselves that a belief that is different from our own might be wrong, but it just might be right. Perhaps we should really get interested in seeking the truth instead of seeking to win an argument with someone who disagrees with us.

One way to improve a little with our PB condition is to decide if the person who has a different opinion from our own is trying to help or is just trying to win an argument or to control us.

Who are some of the people you think of that usually try to help you:

1. _____

2. _____

3. _____

4. _____

5. _____

When you are with those people, consider trying to be a little more OPEN to their ideas. Think of being open the way a flower opens up to the sunlight when it blooms.

Can you picture yourself opening up? Think about your ears taking in the sound of the person's voice. Think about your brain considering the meaning of their words.

Consider yourself responding to a person you disagree with by saying, "Let me think about that" instead of saying, "No, you're wrong."

You may want to practice ending a conversation about new beliefs by saying to the other person, "Thanks for sharing that. I'll think about what you said."

And most of all, remember to be humble, because PB will sometimes happen when you least expect it. What does it mean to be humble? It means to not be too proud or cocky. It means to be courteous and respectful of others. Being humble means remembering that we all still have a lot to learn, and that's okay.

Let's see what you absorbed from this activity about PB. Try answering true or false to these questions. It is okay not to be sure; just do the best you can:

Circle true or false for each statement below:

1. PB stands for Perceptual Blindness.

                                                    True   False

2. Any problem with using our five senses is one kind of PB.

                                                    True   False

3. Another kind of PB is when we don't have the answer to something we need to know.

                                                    True   False

4. Another kind of PB is when we believe something, but our belief is wrong.

                                                    True   False

5. Only a few people have ever had PB because it is very rare.

                                                    True   False

6. One thing we can do to improve our PB is to be cocky and proud and never be humble.

                                                    True   False

7. It can help to think about listening carefully to the people we know who try to help us.

                                                    True   False

8. Being open is like receiving ideas and words the way a flower receives the sunshine as it blooms.

True   False

9. PB is a worldwide handicap because everyone has it sometimes.

True   False

10. Understanding PB might even help me with my counselor.

True   False

Sometimes, kids who have been hurt believe things that are just not true. Their beliefs can make them feel bad about themselves. To help you develop a more positive attitude about yourself, read the Beliefs to Challenge list (on the next page) out loud. Then, read the Beliefs to Practice list out loud. Talk about these lists with a grown-up. You may want to make a copy of the Beliefs to Practice list and put it in a place where you will see it every day.

Beliefs to Challenge

Are these statements really true?

I have to have love and approval from EVERY member of my family and from ALL my friends—even from people who have hurt me.

To be okay as a person, I must never make mistakes and I must do well at everything I try.

When people hurt me, they must be blamed and punished in order for me to be okay again.

I can't stand it if things don't go my way.

Worrying about getting hurt again will prevent it from happening.

I will be happier if I don't think about my problems or bad things that have happened to me.

I can be happier by always depending on others.

What happened to me in the past is the only cause of the problem I have today.

I should feel bad when others feel bad.

I have to find the perfect solution for EVERY problem.

Beliefs to Practice

I can decide whose love and approval I want. Even if I don't get a lot of love and approval, I will still be okay.

I will always try to do my best, and I will remember that mistakes are normal. Other people can do some things better than I can, but there are also things that I can do better than other people. No matter how well I can do something, I will always try to like myself.

People are not perfect, and they sometimes do bad things. Blaming and punishing them will probably not make me feel better, and it may make me feel even worse.

I know that things cannot always go my way, and I won't get upset about that. Worrying does not stop bad things from happening. Instead of worrying, I will think about all the choices I can make and I will pick the best one.

Beliefs to Practice

Ignoring my problems may help me feel better for a while, but it will not solve them and it may even make them worse. Even if it makes me uncomfortable, I will think about my problems and try to solve them.

It is good for me to get help from others when I need it, and I will also work hard to help myself.

How I think now is more important to my feelings than what happened in the past. I will practice having positive and helpful thoughts.

My thoughts or feelings can't change other people's problems, so I won't make myself unhappy by taking on their problems as my own.

I will pick and act on the best solution I can think of, even when it is not perfect.

Head up in the Clouds

When you watch clouds floating by, you have to look up to see them. Looking up is a good thing to do. It makes you hold your head up high, as if you were proud of yourself.

Think about all the things you have to be proud of. Maybe you do well in school. Maybe you help your mom with chores around the house. Coming to counseling to talk about your feelings and what happened is something to be proud of, too! In the clouds below, write all the things you can think of that you are proud of. If you run out of clouds, just draw some more on another piece of paper.

Mamie the Flying Kitten: A Story About Being Yourself

Once upon a time, a little kitten was born in the forest. Her name was Mamie. Mamie's mom could not take care of her, so she left Mamie asleep on the warm, mossy forest floor. As Mamie slept, a kind mama owl saw that she was all alone. Mama Owl knew that this little one would not survive in the forest alone, so she stood watch until Mamie woke up. After a while, the kitten's eyes opened and she realized she had been asleep for a long time. In front of her was a strange-looking animal with feathers and big, brown eyes. Mamie asked the animal her name.

"My name is Mama Owl," she said calmly.

"Are you my mother?" asked Mamie.

"I will be your mother now," Mama Owl answered.

Because Mamie's mother had left so quickly after she was born, Mamie did not really remember her. Mama Owl was the only mother she knew. Now owls and cats are very different, and Mama Owl only knew how to be an owl mother. So she flew up to her nest, carefully carrying little Mamie in her claws. The nest was very different from what Mamie had expected. It was very high, and there were other babies in it. It was quite crowded, but everyone tried to make the best of it.

With Mamie and her other babies safe in the nest, Mama Owl left to search for food. Shortly afterward, she returned with a snake for breakfast. The baby owls were excited about this wonderful meal, but all Mamie could say was "Yuck!" She did not want to eat snakes.

As the days went by, Mama Owl brought all kinds of things for her babies to eat. None of it was what Mamie thought she should eat. But soon, the growling of her empty stomach made her decide she had better eat what Mama Owl brought. So she did.

One day, when the baby owls started to get bigger, Mama Owl told them they would have to learn to fly. Mamie could see that she did not have feathers like Mama Owl or her owl brothers and sisters, but Mama Owl expected her to learn to fly like other owls. The problem was that Mamie was not an owl at all! She was not sure what she was, and no one had ever explained that she was a kitten, not an owl. So Mamie had learned to live in a nest and eat snakes for breakfast, and she was about to try learning to fly. Mamie did not know that kittens are very different from owls—and kittens are not meant to fly.

As the sun came peeking through the clouds, Mamie was nervous because she knew today was flying day. The other owls stretched their wings and fluffed their feathers, getting ready for the big adventure. Mamie had no feathers, so she began to fluff her tail, hoping it would help her fly.

One by one, her owl brothers and sisters took off from the nest to practice their flying. Sometimes, it took a while for them to get the hang of it, but Mama Owl watched out for them. Then it was Mamie's turn. Mamie stood at the edge of the nest and looked down. Though Mamie liked to climb, she did not like looking down. "Go on. You have to fly," Mama Owl told her.

Mamie knew that she was supposed to do what Mama Owl told her to do, but somehow, inside, Mamie knew she was not supposed to fly. She was so scared. Mamie clamped her claws to the edge of the nest and jumped. Down, down, down she went as she flapped her paws and tail. She even tried to flap her ears. Nothing seemed to help Mamie fly, and she fell faster and faster toward the ground. Scared as she was, Mamie kept flapping. Suddenly she stopped falling! Mama Owl had grabbed her and she was flying her back to the nest.

Mamie knew Mama Owl was not happy with her flying. For a long time, Mama Owl was quiet. The other owls were quiet, too, because they did not know what to do. Finally, Mama Owl said "Mamie, you have to learn to fly," and she pushed her toward the edge of the nest. Once again, Mamie jumped from the nest. Paws and tail flapping, she still fell toward the ground, and Mama Owl had to come get her once more. Time and time again, she tried to do what Mama Owl told her and what she thought she was supposed to do. Time and time again, Mamie knew it did not feel right—but she did it anyway.

Now there was a very wise cougar in the forest that day, and she had seen Mamie trying to fly. On one of Mamie's trips down from the nest, Mama Owl flew to the ground with her, rather than taking her back to the nest. When they landed, Mamie jumped around, glad to have her feet on the ground but disappointed she had not done what Mama Owl had told her to. It just so happened that they landed right by the cougar.

"My, that sure was a sight," said the cougar, laughing.

"What are you talking about?" Mamie asked, seeing that the cougar was friendly.

"You!" the cougar explained. "I've never seen a cat try to fly like a bird before."

Mamie was surprised, because she did not know she was a cat. She did not even know what a cat was. She just thought she was a funny-looking owl.

"What did you call me?" Mamie asked the cougar.

"A cat. You're a cat like me, only different," the cougar said.

"I'm not a cat; I'm an owl," Mamie said, as she fluffed up her fur.

"You're a cat trying to be an owl, but you, my little friend, are definitely a cat," the cougar told her.

"I don't believe you," Mamie said.

"Well, let's take a look at the evidence and then decide," remarked the cougar, as she walked around Mamie, looking at her carefully.

Mamie was a little bit frightened because the cougar was so much bigger, but Mama Owl was close by, listening to every word.

"Let's start at the top," said the cougar. "You have whiskers, and owls do not have whiskers."

Sure enough, Mamie ran her paws beside her nose and found … whiskers! She had never noticed them before, and Mama Owl had no whiskers.

"Then there's the stuff covering your body. It's called fur. Not feathers like Mama Owl, but fur like me," said the cougar, as she licked her own fur.

"Still, I don't look like you, so I'm not a cat," Mamie shouted

"No, you don't look like me, 'cause I'm a big cat," the cougar replied, standing up to her full height. "You are a kitten, a little cat, a baby cat."

As Mamie looked at the cougar and then at herself, she had to agree. From their paws to their tails, they looked a lot alike. For perhaps the first time in her life, Mamie took a good, long look at Mama Owl. Again, she looked at herself. It was true; she and Mama Owl were not at all alike. Mamie had lived in a nest high in the tree, she had eaten snakes for breakfast, and she had tried to fly—but she was still not like Mama Owl. She finally realized who she was. Mamie was a cat.

Knowing who she was, Mamie was finally free to be herself, and she stopped trying to be something she wasn't. Mama Owl had done her best to take care of Mamie, but she hadn't known how to help Mamie be what she was meant to be. Mama Owl would always be special to her, but now Mamie knew who she really was.

In the weeks that followed, Mamie learned more and more about herself. The cougar helped her learn what it meant to be a cat, and Mamie grew to understand how special she was. One day, walking by the pond, Mamie stopped and looked at her reflection in the sparkling water. She smiled, as she looked carefully at every part of the beautiful, furry creature looking back at her.

"I am Mamie the cat," she said, "and I am special." Mamie smiled as she walked away, knowing she had become exactly what she was meant to be. Never again would she let herself try to be anything that she was not meant to be.

Sharon A. McGee, LMFT, LPC-S, RPT, is a therapist who works with children, adolescents, and adults. Sharon has specialized in the field of trauma recovery for more than twenty years and currently maintains a private practice in Montgomery, AL. She is also a freelance author.

Curtis Holmes, Ph.D., is a psychologist who has been in practice for over thirty years. After studying school psychology and clinical psychology at the University of Georgia, he practiced as a school psychologist for three years in rural South Carolina, and then went on to practice as a clinical psychologist at a large mental health facility in Louisville, KY. Since 1977, he has been in private practice in Georgia, where he specializes in the assessment and treatment of child sexual abuse survivors, family members, and offenders.

more instant help books

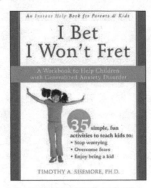

I BET I WON'T FRET

A Workbook to Help
Children with Generalized
Anxiety Disorder

US $16.95 / ISBN: 978-1-572246003

THE RELAXATION &
STRESS REDUCTION
WORKBOOK FOR KIDS

Help for Children to Cope with
Stress, Anxiety & Transitions

US $16.95 / ISBN: 978-1572245822

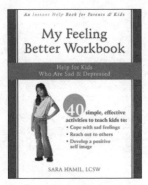

MY FEELING BETTER
WORKBOOK

Help for Kids Who Are
Sad & Depressed

US $16.95 / ISBN: 978-1572246126

WHAT'S EATING YOU?

A Workbook for Teens with Anorexia,
Bulimia & other Eating Disorders

US $14.95 / ISBN: 978-1572246072

STOPPING THE PAIN

A Workbook for Teens who
Cut & Self-Injure

US $14.95 / ISBN: 978-1572246027

Instant Help Books
A Division of New Harbinger Publications, Inc.

available from

new**harbinger**publications, inc.

and fine booksellers everywhere

To order, call toll free **1-800-748-6273** or visit our online
bookstore at **www.newharbinger.com**

(VISA, MC, AMEX / prices subject to change without notice)